Tak' a Bowl o' Brose
for Breakfast,

Kail and Tatties
when ye can:

Sup yer Parritch
like yer faither,

If ye want to be a man.

Allan Junior.

No. 186.

A Bowl of
PORRIDGE

SCOTS WHA HA'E.

Guthrie Hutton

Argyll
publishing

© Guthrie Hutton 2005

First published in 2005 by
Argyll Publishing
Glendaruel
Argyll PA22 3AE
Scotland
www.argyllpublishing.com

The author has asserted his moral rights.

**British Library Cataloguing-in-Publication Data.
A catalogue record for this book is available
from the British Library.**

ISBN 1 902831 79 9

Cover photo: stockscotland.com

Origination: Cordfall Ltd, Glasgow

Printing: Cromwell Press Ltd

Introduction

In his *Dictionary of the English Language*, published in 1755, Dr Samuel Johnson famously defined oats as:

> 'A grain, which in England is generally given to horses, but in Scotland supports the people'.

If he intended to rile the Scots, he succeeded. Outraged defenders rounded on him with the riposte that this resulted in better men and better horses (which was true). But while this may have assuaged wounded egos it could not disguise the hard reality that lay behind the Scots' consumption of oats. For the peasantry of highlands and lowlands, oatmeal was the principal foodstuff, and it was even used as a form of payment for poor labourers. People ate it because they had to. They had little else.

It went into soups, mealy puddings and the haggis, but principally it was used to make oatcakes, oat bread, bannocks, brose, gruel, sowens and of course porridge. Johnson's definition of porridge was less controversial: 'food made by boiling meat in water; broth'.

In Scotland oatmeal was often called meat and

Rabbie Burns's description of the haggis as 'great chieftain o' the puddin' race' is well known, but Burns also penned an accolade for porridge in The Cottar's Saturday Night calling it 'The halesome Porritch, chief of Scotia's food'.

porridge was indeed meal thickened in a pot of boiling water. People also varied this basic dish, and even used different words and spellings for it. So it was potage, parritch, parridge, porritch, or in Gaelic, brochan. Gruel, brose and sowans were also made by mixing oatmeal and water, as were some regional variations with strange sounding names like blerie, bluthrie, gogar, lewlands, milgruel, willins and others.

Porridge can of course be made with other grains and is found in the cuisine of almost every country. The Chinese make a rice porridge called Congee and the Norwegian Rommegrot, or creamed porridge, is made with sour cream, milk, flour and salt. In times of hardship people have made porridge with stale bread, and even in Scotland it was made with barley, or peas and beans before oats were adopted as the dominant grain. So the Scots have pulled off a remarkable trick by getting the rest of the world to recognise oatmeal porridge as the one true porridge, and to regard it as uniquely Scottish.

Poetry and Parritch

Postcards published
1890s/early 1900s which
show the universal
appeal of porridge in
Scotland across the
class divide

Waiter's Smile.

If Quaker Oats the order be
This waiter's sure he'll get a fee,
And so upon his face we see
The smile that won't come off!

Mechanised harvesting of oats c. 1905

GROWING THE OATS

The common oat (*avena sativa*) appears to have been developed from wild grasses found in Asia and eastern Europe, and was known to early civilisations in the Middle East, Greece and Rome. It was used mainly as animal feed although the Greeks are thought to have been the first to make a porridge with it. Oat cultivation moved west across Europe and may have reached the British Isles by about the Iron Age (c.400-250 BC). In the north of these islands, the grain found a climate much to its liking.

Oats grow slowly in cold, wet conditions which allow the kernels to swell and fill out, whereas the more rapid growth in warmer climes results in smaller, thinner grains. The cereal can also prosper in poorer earth – Scotland and oat it seems were soil mates!

Early plants were probably not much different from

the original wild grasses, but over the years plant husbandry perfected a number of different strains: Abundance, Onward, Star, Victory and others. One of the most common varieties was the Potato Oat which was apparently found growing on a dung heap in a Cumberland potato field, in 1788. The dung gave it vigour, the field, its name!

Oats were sown in spring – as early as February if conditions permitted – on ground which had been ploughed in the autumn. There was often no break in cereal production with oats and barley (also known as bere or bear) being rotated over a two or three year cycle. Some plots were used year after year without preparation until they had to be set aside to recover from exhaustion, but yields improved as the riggs of early husbandry were replaced by larger fields, and practices like fertilisation and rotation were better understood.

Harvesting methods too improved over time with sickle and scythe being replaced progressively by reaper/binder and, the ultimate development of agricultural machinery, the combine harvester. The older methods, including binders, were better for oats than combine harvesters. These giant machines tend to waste grain in pursuit of speed and have contributed to a decline in oat

Uncle Ebenezer, in Robert Louis Stevenson's
Kidnapped, described porridge as: 'fine, halesome
food — they're grand food, parritch.'

cultivation because barley is easier to combine. They have
also done away with those evocative countryside images
of stooks in the fields and stacks in the farmyard, but have
eased the burden of long days and heavy work that fell on
the farming community at harvest time.

A successful harvest for pre-machine farming folk was
such a relief that they set about the serious business of
celebrating with music, merriment and strong drink. More
sober thanksgivings were played out at church harvest
festivals, but before the crop could fulfil its promise, the
oats had to be milled into meal.

Restored water mill at Blair Atholl, Perthshire

THE MILL AND THE MEAL

Before milling, the grain had to be dried – 'kilned' or 'toasted' – and the slower this was done, the better the flavour. It was then passed through 'shelling stones' – mill stones that only cracked the skins off the groats – the kernels of the grain.

Skin and groats were separated from each other by winnowing which, in the past, was done by throwing them in the air and allowing the wind to blow away the skins, while the heavier groats fell to the ground. A wise winnower spread a cloth on the ground to catch them. The shelled groats were then passed through another set of mill stones which ground them into different grades of meal – pinhead, coarse (these are sometimes spoken of as being the same), medium or fine.

Iron-age oat eaters milled their grain by placing it on a flat or concave stone and beating it with another, like using a mortar and pestle. This technique developed with the grain being crushed by a cylindrical stone being rolled along a slightly concave one and, by turning this action on its side, the hand-operated mill, known as a 'quern',

Highland nostalgia: the handmill or quern

The Handmill.

evolved. These mini-mills were introduced to Scotland *c*.80 AD and were still in use up to comparatively recent times. They consisted of two flat stones, up to two feet in diameter. The lower one was sometimes lipped to contain the upper which had a hole in it so that grain could be poured between the stones. It was rotated using a wooden handle.

Over time, larger mills were developed. These could be driven by animals, wind or tide, but water was the primary source of power in Scotland. Water mills were a big investment and so 'thirlage', a system of financing them, was developed. The landowners – lairds, or on church lands abbots – built the mills, part-paid the millers, and guaranteed a supply of grain by tying or 'thirling' the tenancies of peasant farmers to the mill. These ties also prohibited the farmers from hand-milling their own grain (although it didn't stop them), and they had to keep the mill, dam and lade in a good state of repair. The superior was also entitled to a proportion of the ground meal, and some of the meal also went to the millers.

Thirlage may have seemed necessary at first, but over time it encouraged disputes and caused resentment summed up in a bitter little saying:

Variations on the phrase 'Save your breath to
cool your porridge' were borrowed from
Plutarch by Sir Walter Scott in Old Mortality
and George Bernard Shaw in Saint Joan.

'ane tae graw, ane tae gnaw and ane to pay the
laird withaw'.

Evasion, or attempts to give the superior short-measure,
were commonplace, and millers were often suspected of
cheating and became distrusted social outcasts. The system
only started to disappear when farmers became less reliant
on oats, although some had to buy themselves out to be
free of it.

Once people had their meal they had to find a way of
keeping it before use. Oatmeal can absorb moisture and
thus lose flavour, or take on a bitter taste unless kept in a
dry, airtight container. People therefore preferred freshly
ground meal, but had to store their grain so that it did not
deteriorate. This was done in a chest known as a girnal in
which the grain had to be tamped down as tightly as
possible to keep out damp and air. Mice also had to be
discouraged although the line in an old Scots greeting –

'May the mouse ne'er leave your girnal
wi' a tear drap in its e'e'

– might suggest a recognition of shared struggle with
another of God's creatures.

One of a series of advertising 'smiles' that was probably closer to historical reality than Quaker's ad-men realised. Tramps, known as gaberlunzies, went from door to door begging for oatmeal which they kept in a satchel, or wallet, slung around their necks.

Tramp's Smile.

This tramp got at a garden gate
Some Quaker Oats—"Well, ain't that great!"
See o'er his features radiate
The smile that won't come off!

PORRIDGE IN THE PAST

Armies from the Romans onwards have eaten oatmeal. At the Battle of Hastings the French munched oatcakes while the English ate a kind of porridge. That the cake eaters won has not deterred those in charge of British forces from feeding their troops with porridge up to the present day.

Writing in 1327, the chronicler Sir John Froissart was one the first to refer to the Scots and oatmeal when describing their military campaigns:

> They take with them no purveyance of bread or wine for their usage and soberness is such in time of war that they will pass in the journey a great long time with flesh half sodden (half boiled) without bread and drink of the river water without wine and they neither care for pots nor pans for they see the beasts in their own skins. They are ever sure to find plenty of beasts in the country that they will pass through: therefore they carry with them none other purveyance, but on their horse, between the saddle and the panel, they

truss a broad plate of metal (another translation of Froissart describes the utensil as a flat stone) and behind the saddle they will have a little sack of oatmeal, to the extent that when they have eaten of the sodden flesh then they lay this plate on the fire and temper a little of the oatmeal; and when the plate is hot, they cast of the thin paste thereon and make a little cake in a manner of a cracknell or biscuit, and that they eat to comfort withall their stomachs. Wherefore it is no great marvel though they make greater journeys than other people do.

These warriors may of course have been doing what Scots on more peaceable pursuits did every day. Certainly the pattern they set was perpetuated in following centuries by cattle drovers who carried oatmeal and, when they stopped for a rest, made oatcakes and bannocks. Sometimes they bled an animal to mix the blood with oatmeal and make a more nutritious cake.

Students took a sack of oatmeal when they went to college and eked out the contents until a mid-term holiday – Mealy Monday – allowed them time to go home to collect another sack. This traditional holiday was still being

Porridge features in a number of little sayings:
'There would be little parritch in your cup if he had the pouring of it!' (meanness)
'As plain as parritch.' (clear as crystal)
'Back tae auld claes and parritch.' (down to earth)

observed at St Andrews University up to the start of the twenty first century.

Hugh Miller, the nineteenth century Cromarty stonemason, describing the life of itinerant masons, wrote of men crowded into a bothy at the end of a working day. Some were: 'baking and firing oaten cakes', while others were 'cooking their evening porridge'.

Up to the mid-twentieth century, North East farm labourers in their primitive bothies, scrounged what they could, but basically lived on porridge. The youngest usually made it and, if inexperienced in the art of sprinkling oatmeal into the boiling water, created knots (oaten lumps)

The theme of the student, the farm labourer, or the adventurer setting off with nothing but a bag of meal on his back is an established part of Scottish folklore

The 'Back Bone' of a Scotchman

swimming in a thin gruel. The abuse of fellow workers quickly turned raw laddies into experts. Somehow these bothy men survived to tell the tale, despite the practice of simply wiping their bowls clean, on dirty trousers, and allowing a crust of old porridge to build up around the rim.

Before the bothy culture developed, farm hands were provided with food, a practice that continued on at least one Kirkcudbrightshire farm into the twentieth century. There the farmer's wife made a communal pot of porridge which she began to cook the previous night and then, by putting it in a box surrounded by straw, it continued to

THE CROFTER'S GRACE.

'Doing porridge', the convicts' alternative term for a prison sentence,

cook through the night. It was taken out in the morning and the hands sat around the table, each with a bowl of milk, and they scooped porridge from the area of the pot nearest to them, dipping each spoonful in the milk before eating it. The cooking method gave the porridge such a firm consistency that each man was able to create his own scooped out area surrounded by an unbroken wall of porridge. Any that was not eaten was fed to the dogs.

In the home, porridge remained the principal dish for breakfast and supper, although people tried to vary their diet. St Kildans boiled a puffin with oatmeal to give flavour to their porridge, or made a porridge by mixing

Images of Scots and their porridge:
The Crofter's Grace (opposite)– this frugal scene of the crofter and his bowl of porridge was used to illustrate the Grace:

Some hae meat that cannot eat
And some there be that want it.
But we hae meat and we can eat,
And sae the Lord be thankit.
by Rabbie Burns

oatmeal with the juice of a boiled fulmar.

A poor eighteenth century household could start the day with porridge or brose, have a dinner of kale broth with bannocks washed down with ale or milk, and there was more porridge with sowans or kale for supper.

One Banffshire farm hand's family in the 1840s started the day with oatmeal porridge served with skimmed milk; potatoes and salt, or oatcakes with skimmed milk, sufficed for lunch; supper was boiled greens with kale brose – oatmeal stirred in the boiling water in which the greens had been boiled.

Brose or gruel were made by stirring boiling water or hot milk into a bowl of oatmeal, and if wanted, other ingredients like fruit or nuts, could be mixed in too. Sowans was made by stirring oatmeal and water together, leaving the mixture for a few days until it was turning sour, and then draining the thinner parts off and boiling them to make a light pudding.

Without oats people could starve and when crops failed, famines ensued. These tended to last for two years because people had to eat their seed grain in the first bad year, and suffer the consequences the year after. Between 1695 and 1699 Scotland suffered a terrible shortage. It foreshadowed events in Ireland in the 1840s when similar

The so-called 'Battle Hymn of the Army Catering Corps', first spoken by broadcaster Willie Rushton, included these lines:
But cook is deaf to insults, he's never yet heard praise
Be it curry for the Ghurkas, or porridge for the Greys

dependence on a single crop, the potato, led to famine. Popular history has chosen to remember the Irish suffering while ignoring the Scottish oat failure, but the result was the same: high mortality, increased poverty, emigration (paradoxically to Ireland) and begging.

The famine undermined the country's shaky economy before the disastrous failure of the colonial settlement at Darien, near present day Panama, weakened it further and persuaded the Scots' parliament to pass the Act of Union in 1707. So it is not entirely flippant to suggest that a shortage of porridge had an influence on the decision to unify Scotland and England.

Potatoes, which could have alleviated the famine, were introduced to Ireland in the late sixteenth century, but the Scots were slow to adopt this dubious import. Their conservativism was encouraged by churchmen who thought that potatoes were an unfit food because the Bible did not mention them.

For poor people, oatmeal remained the main part of a meagre diet up to the second half of the nineteenth century. The long, dark days of Winter were always difficult, but the worst season was Spring when the meal was running low.

The corn exchange, a market where grain was bought and sold, was a feature of many towns. Leith's was one of the most important. It traded in imports though the docks, and the best of home-grown produce from Mid and East Lothian.

England's national bard, William Shakespeare, in Act II, Scene 1 of The Tempest when Sebastian says of Gonzalo: 'He receives comfort like cold porridge'

A lack of systems to control supplies and prices compounded seasonal uncertainties for urban Scots. There were food riots in Glasgow in 1763, at a time when there was plenty of meal. It happened because farmers and traders brought so much meal to the market the price fell to a point where neither could afford to sell. Poor people, who had been hoping prices would fall further, were left stranded. Convinced that traders were storing meal to inflate the price, they persuaded the city magistrates to inspect the warehouses, but when no stockpiles were found, the mob went on the rampage. Traders hid, or ran for their lives, as their houses and shops were ransacked by people high on looted whisky.

Edinburgh also had riots following a five-day period when there was meal in the shops, but none in the market at prices poor people could afford. There were riots in Dundee and other east coast ports in the late eighteenth and early nineteenth centuries when people saw grain being shipped out. They were suspicious that shortages elsewhere were encouraging merchants to export grain to places where they could get a higher price. This in turn would create a shortage where the grain had come from, causing the price to rise there. But while the merchants made money, the urban poor faced starvation.

In better-off households porridge appears to have been eaten less and less, and even breakfast took on a different aspect. This trend appears to have developed during the eighteenth century and taken hold in polite society during that great period of cultural advancement, the Scottish Enlightenment.

Visitors to Scotland at the time, found breakfasts memorable and even Dr Johnson, whose barb about the Scots and their oats caused such offence, was moved to declare:

> in the breakfast, the Scots . . . must be confessed
> to excel us (the English).

He is just one of a number of writers quoted by F. Marian McNeill, the doyen of Scottish cookery writers, in *The Scots Kitchen: Its Traditions and Lore With Old-Time Recipes* published in 1929. The descriptions she found from the early part of the eighteenth century spoke of 'priestly' ham, 'knightly' sirloin, 'baron' of beef, venison pasties and toast, washed down with ale, mead, wine or spirits. Some later scribes bemoaned the passing of these delights, while others applauded the foods that replaced them: tea, coffee, warm bread, rolls, biscuits, oatcakes, butter, honey, conserves, marmalades, cheeses, eggs, salted

Noel Coward wrote in his satire 'The English Lido':
There's sand in the porridge and sand in the bed
And if this is pleasure we'd rather be dead.

or smoked meats, smoked salmon, finnan haddie and salt herring. Of all the quoted writers, however, only two referred to porridge.

This great Scottish breakfast was still being praised in Victorian times when novelist Henry Kingsley wrote:

'brother, let us breakfast in Scotland, lunch in Australia and dine in Paris'.

The meal, however, had degenerated into a culinary disaster by 1907 when *The Glasgow Herald* reported a German doctor's views on the fare offered at hotels and guest houses. He described fried ham and eggs as the 'curse of Scotland', found finnan haddie 'loathsome' and was appalled at the notion of 'decorating' it with a poached egg. Warming to his theme, the doctor claimed that the Scottish male did not eat what he wanted, but what the wife, mother, or landlady put before him. On this evidence, breakfasts of ham, eggs, fish, chops or steak were a sinister plot designed to get rid of the man for the whole day and, because no-one could stomach such fare unless habituated to it over a long time, such a tactic could not have developed overnight. The article was written in July when 'strawberries and salad' could have provided a light, wholesome breakfast, but curiously for a newspaper staunchly supportive of all things Scottish, in many column inches of close set type, there was no mention of porridge.

It seems that middle-class breakfasts had not featured porridge for almost two centuries, while the rural poor ate little else, but what of the industrial poor? Did they eat porridge in the ritualistic way that modern cookbooks describe, or did they adopt different breakfasting habits?

Scotland's industrial revolution began in 1760 with the great Carron Ironworks. It was followed by factories, foundries, mills, mines and shipyards that transformed the country's economy from a largely rural one to one based on industry. Despite this, descriptions of the nation's eating habits tend to reflect only the landed classes or country people as if industry didn't exist. It did, and it involved the vast majority of the population through the nineteenth and early twentieth centuries.

The owners of the cotton mill at New Lanark took their social responsibilities more seriously than most and provided their workers with oatmeal porridge or sowans, with milk. New Lanark's owners were of course famously paternalistic, but was this just an act of benevolence or were the workers kept so busy they had no time to prepare their own food? That question begs another: if working people were too busy to cook, was a dish like porridge,

The boy crying for his porridge and the image of eager eating were common cartoon themes at a time – the early twentieth century – when porridge eating was in decline.
The adulterating of good meal with inferior produce, or even sawdust, was a concern that spanned centuries.

which took time to prepare, as common in the homes of the industrial poor as in those of the rural poor?

An article in the mill trade journal, *The Miller*, in 1890, provides a clue. It suggested that all was not well in the meal trade in the nation's industrial capital, Glasgow, where the population was increasing rapidly, while oatmeal sales remained static; in effect a reduction. The writer suggested:

> 'this falling off may be accounted for by . . . the great distances that many of the labouring classes are from their place of abode at meal times, the limited amount of time that is allowed for meals, and the length of time that is required for the preparation of a dish of good porridge.

He underlined the problem by pointing to the 'enormous increase in the consumption of loaf bread in recent years'.

Porridge, it seems, had met its nemesis. Wheat flour and industrial bakeries had proliferated during this period of industrial expansion, creating an easy breakfast – a slice of toast – and an easy snack, the sandwich. And there was no washing up – porridge did not just take time to prepare, but in the days before non-stick pans and dishwashers, it took time and effort to wash up!

This rapid change to an urban, industrial society was huge, and many of the old ways were swept up into a nostalgic, tartan-wrapped image of the past. Porridge began to appear in recipe books as 'invalid food' and a letter to the *Fifeshire Journal* in 1873 revealed:

> 'oatmeal porridge is excellent food for growing children, though it may not be quite the fashion for young ladies'.

Was porridge being consigned to the sick room and nursery, and did it simply become unfashionable?

A late nineteenth century advertisement for Quaker Oats which were rolled oats or oat flakes. Rolled oats meant huge changes in the meal trade.

Quaker Oats.

QUAKER OATS is a Pure Cereal Food made from choice white oats.

It can be quickly cooked for Breakfast, is delicious, healthful, and economical.

Three pounds of QUAKER OATS cost less than one pound of beef, and it is three times as nutritious per pound.

Highest Award, World's Fair, 1893.

TRADE MARK.

An Ideal Health Food for Children. Gives them rosy cheeks, strong nerves, and good teeth.

Ask your Grocer for it.

Sold in 2-lb. Packages only.

ARMSTRONG & CO., LITH. BOSTON.

PORRIDGE IN A PACKET

If porridge consumption was slowing in Scotland, the pace was quickening in America, and 'quick' was the watchword. One of the men credited with this was John Stuart, a Scot who had emigrated to Canada in 1850. He began milling oats there, but moved to Cedar Rapids, Iowa, where in 1877 he and some other millers teamed up to establish the Quaker Mill Company. A few years later the company was selling rolled oats which were made by cutting the oat into three, and then steaming these pieces to cook them and gelatinise the starch before putting them through rollers to flatten them into flakes.

Meanwhile, in 1886 in Britain, while Scotland's oat millers were lamenting the slow-down in their trade and the demise of the old ways, the new Caledonian Oatmeal Mills (of Carlisle, England!) started to market a new kind of meal which they called 'oat-flake'. *The Miller* reporter's verdict on the new product was that it made 'a delicious porridge, of sufficient body, and yet eating sweet and crisp'.

Not that the idea of crushing oats between rollers was new; it had been around since the mid-seventeenth

Cupar Mills in the days of TD Drummond

century when it was found that oats treated in this way were more nourishing to horses. But now, with advances in the technique being made in the USA and south of the border, Scotland was facing a major challenge to its primacy in porridge making.

That challenge escalated either side of the First World War with large quantities of rolled oats and oatmeal coming into the country from Germany. Without modern plant Scotland's millers could not compete on price, and the competition got close and personal. Quaker had set up a British operation in 1899, initially to import the parent company's products from America, but in 1936 a mill was established at Southall, close to the London docks. It was soon producing a range of cereal products for the British market. Scottish producers relied on the quality of their product to see them through.

The Inverurie-based North of Scotland Milling Company marketed their 'Grampian' oat products on the basis that Scotch oatmeal and rolled oats 'make the finest porridge and go further than . . . other oats'. This was echoed by Robert Robinson & Son of Annan in

Barry Milll, Angus, now owned by National Trust for Scotland

Dumfriess-shire who dismissed the transatlantic threat. Their advertisements claimed that two packets of their Provost Oats would 'make as much porridge as three packets of American' and asserted that there were 'no oats like Scotch oats and no Scotch oats like Provost Oats'.

Quaker simply hammered home their message with a single word, 'Quick'.

'The best that Mummy can buy' was the slogan used by the Angus Milling Company to market their Peter Pan Scotch Oats. The company was based at Kirriemuir and identified its product with the most famous character invented by J.M.Barrie, the town's most famous author. It was tricky to promote because Peter Pan never grew old, and this conflicted with the message that children who ate porridge would grow up healthy and strong!

The company was set up in the late 1930s when the tennant of the Meikle Mill, J.A. Whamond and Sons Ltd, bought the mill from the landowner. After the Second World War large companies began to buy-up smaller mills and, with demand falling, closed these and concentrated production on larger ones. New owners took over the

Hunter & Sons of Murrayfield Mills in Edinburgh was one of the largest companies trading on the quality of Miidlothian oats. And as this early 1900s advert shows they were also trading in rolled oats

BEGIN THE DAY WELL, BY TAKING PORRIDGE MADE WITH HUNTER'S FAMED OATMEAL OR OATENA (ROLLED OATS)

Angus Milling Company, and the North of Scotland Milling Company. They also joined forces with Hamlyn & Co. who had bought Cupar Mills, in Fife, from T.D. Drummond in 1944. Further company take-overs saw the 'Peter Pan' name dropped in the 1970s in favour of 'Hamlyn's' and the closure of the Kirriemuir operation in 1991. The Hamlyn's brand name, however, has survived other ownership changes and is still produced at a large new mill at Boyndie in Banffshire.

Perhaps the biggest concentration of late nineteenth and early twentieth century mills was in and around Edinburgh where they capitalised on the premier status of Midlothian oats. These included Hunter & Son's Murrayfield Mills, John Inglis & Sons' Midlothian Oatmeal Mills at Leith and Junction Mill, Leith, a former Inglis mill operated by the Scottish Co-operative Wholesale Society. James Pendreich & Son made their 'Heart of Midlothian' oatmeal at the Catcune Mills, Gorebridge and Robert Smith produced 'Edinburgh Oatmeal' at the West Mills, Midcalder.

Another company trading on the fame of Midlothian oats, A&R Scott, actually started in Glasgow c.1880. They made Scott's Midlothian Oat Flour, oatcakes and oat flour biscuits at this western base, before moving to the West Mills at Colinton on the Water of Leith in 1909. Scotts Porage Oats – the spelling of 'porage' was registered as a trade mark – was first marketed in 1914 and ten years later the famous shot-putting highlander appeared on the packaging. So too, at times, did the words 'Cooks in Five Minutes' and the slogan 'The Food of a Mighty Race'. In order to expand after the Second World War, in 1947, they bought a redundant flax mill at Cupar, in Fife. It was used to produce rolled oats, and these have continued to be made at the plant through company take-overs in the 1960s by, first, Cerebos and then Rank Hovis McDougal. In 1970/71 Colinton Mill was closed and Cupar expanded, and in 1982 the A&R Scott business was taken over again; this time by Quaker Oats Ltd – the wheel had come full circle.

The large Cupar and Boyndie plants, and smaller mills at Kelso and Alford, maintain Scotland's place as a centre for milling oats, but large mills also operate in Northern Ireland and England where Mornflake Oats claim to have started milling at Crewe, in Cheshire, in 1675, and are still going strong. A number of old water-mills have also been put back into working order. Some of

Scott's Porage Oats delivery van from 1951
(Photo: courtesy Robert Grieves)

these are open to visitors and offer their own brand of oatmeal, and recipes for porridge, to people who want to sample the real thing.

The advent of rolled oats (and there are now Jumbo oatflakes made with the whole groat) had a big effect on the way people thought about porridge. The heat treatment inevitably took away some flavour and nutrients, and the end result may not have satisfied discerning traditionalists, but for people thirled to a factory or office routine they made porridge possible. And they still meet modern demands on time, especially when allied to technological advances like non-stick pans and microwave ovens. Indeed a whole new range of flavoured porridge products is now being made for the microwave market.

HEALTHY COMPETITION

In recent years a vast array of heavily advertised convenience breakfast foods has appeared in the shops. Their colourful packaging, hyped-up health claims and 'free' plastic giveaways are all designed to tempt the customer, but porridge is fighting back with promotional activities of its own.

In 1994 the Carrbridge Community Council held the first World Porridge Making Championships. The idea was devised (by an Englishman) to give the village a boost at the end of the tourist season and since then, with sponsorship from Hamlyns, it has become a porridge festival with other activities taking place alongside the main event.

Over the years newspaper reporters and television presenters have joined the contestants, who come from near and far to compete for the title of 'Master Porridge Maker' and the coveted Golden Spurtle Challenge Trophy. They parade through the village folllowed by a throng of onlookers who file into the community hall to watch the contest (porridge-making as a spectator sport, now that is remarkable!). Rolled oats are not permitted, only oatmeal, and the contestants supply their own ingredients, including the water. Heats are followed by a cook-off and after a final tasting the judges emerge with a victor.

A similar event, sponsored by Scott's Porage Oats, is held as part of St Andrews Week in the town's Byre Theatre. While contestants from local hotels and guest houses go through their culinary routines, the audience is entertained by a host who talks to or, more accurately, distracts the chefs and teases the public in equal measure. The event is therefore more of an entertainment than the Carrbridge contest, but like it the winner's trophy is a golden spurtle.

These events are fun, but the real trump card in the porridge arsenal is that it is a healthy food. The Scots instinctively knew this. Longevity was put down to a daily helping of porridge and if someone showed physical weakness or weariness they would be ribbed for not having eaten their porridge that morning. There was, however, one small cloud: an unrelieved diet of oatmeal was thought to cause the 'scotch fiddle', a skin complaint which made people itch, but nobody really knew the cause and so people kept on eating oats.

A wartime leaflet issued in the 1940s by
John Inglis & Sons to promote the
healthy nature of their products

Written evidence supported the oral beliefs. A cookbook published by the *People's Friend* in 1877 started with its recipe for porridge:

> 'The laxative and regulative qualities of good oatmeal are well known . . . porridge in fact ought to be a regular article of diet in every family, as an antidote to indigestion, and a saving in the way of doctor's bills'.

Oatmillers Grants of Dundee suggested in a pamphlet, in 1883, that:

> 'when tried by . . . chemical analysis . . . oats are proved to be the most nutritious of all cereals'.

In an article in 1922, Mary MacKirdy, a cookery writer for *The Glasgow Herald*, extolled the 'high nutrative value' of oatmeal and suggested that 'its use should be encouraged, not only for porridge and oatcakes'. And when Edinburgh's former Medical Officer of Health, Dr. William Robertson MD, supported these claims in the 1940s, people could feel comfortable with what they knew to be correct.

Further confirmation came in 1981 when a team of scientists at the University of Kentucky College of Medicine reported that they had 'discovered' (discovered! – the cheek of them) this wonder food with amazing health-

UNEQUALLED FOR
INFANTS, CHILDREN, & INVALIDS.
SCOTT'S
Midlothian
OAT-FLOUR

EIGHT First-Class Exhibition Awards.
Highly Recommended by the Medical Profession.

Porridge as health food – Scott's trading on the healthy properties of oats in 1888

giving properties. They found that porridge contained a gummy fibre material which could reduce cholesterol, regulate blood sugar and fats, and be beneficial to those suffering from diabetes, heart disease and hypertension.

Science also showed that oatmeal was rich in *inositol*, one of the B complex vitamins found in high concentration in the heart and the lens of the eye – confirming the belief, long held on the west coast of Scotland, that porridge was good for the eyes. More of these vital B vitamins are contained in oats than in any other cereals with *thiamine*, *riboflavin*, *niacin* and *pyridoxine* present. Also present is the heart vitamin, vitamin E *tocopherol*.

Oats are also rich in minerals including calcium and phosphorous – for bones and teeth; potassium – for muscle cells and blood corpuscles; iron – for haemoglobin and copper – for red blood cells. Almost three-quarters of the oat is made up of carbohydrate – essential for energy – and the other quarter is split 60-40 between protein – for growth – and a balance of polyunsaturated and saturated fatty acids.

Oatmeal and porridge also have value when taken externally. People with skin conditions like excema or psoriasis can ease their suffering by taking a bath in water which has been run through oatmeal. Likewise people needing a poultice could use this 1940s recipe from the *Dundee Homecraft Book*:

1. Make thick porridge and spread on piece of soft thin cloth, fold over edges and place between two hot plates and carry to patient.
2. Apply gently and cover well to keep heat in.
3. Remove when cool and dry skin; then cover with cotton wool.

The positive science was of course good news for oat growers and millers, as was the rise in popularity of another breakfast food – muesli. Devised in the early twentieth century by a Swiss physician, Dr Max Bircher-Benner, muesli consisted of apple, hazelnuts, lemon juice, sultanas and of course milk added to a base of rolled oats. If this sounds familiar, it is because, apart from a couple of extras, muesli and brose are quite similar. The Scots seemed to have missed a trick, although by concentrating on porridge the nation has transformed it into a totemic image of the country. All that remains is to cook it and eat it.

Fat tummies were perhaps not the
healthy image porridge producers
wished to promote!

An iron pot hanging on a chain from a swee over an open fire may have appealed to a romantic view of the past, But it was not a convenient way to cook breakfast in the modern age.

"making Parritch"

COOKING and EATING

The ingredients for making oatmeal porridge are simple: oatmeal, a coarse or medium texture is best to prevent the finished product becoming slimy or sludgy, salt and water. The utensils are simple too; a pot and a stirring stick known as a spurtle or theevil. Tradition requires that porridge should always be stirred clockwise, either to bring good luck, or because going anti-clockwise would provoke the devil.

The Food Question porridge

The Season's Greetings.
With Hearty Good Wishes, and may your Bowl of Happiness be full at this Happy Season.

A lonely Scrooge-like porridge eater with a Christmas message in 1905

When cooked, porridge was served in one bowl, with the cream, milk, or buttermilk in a separate bowl. This was done to keep the porridge hot and the milk cold: the greater the difference in temperature the better the taste and experience. A wooden bowl maintained the heat best, and a horn spoon prevented the mouth from being burned.

In the North-East, porridge left over from the morning and warmed up with hot milk was known as as 'potty-

Charles Dickens, on seeing the gravestone of Edinburgh corn merchant Ebenezer Scroggie, is believed to have misread the words 'meal man' as 'mean man' — an error which apparently inspired the character Ebenezer Scrooge in A Christmas Carol

porridge', elsewhere it was 'calders'. People also poured left-over porridge into a 'drawer' and let it go cold, and solid. When wanted it was sliced, like bread is today. In later years people ate slices of cold porridge on toast, or floured and fried them as part of a cooked breakfast.

A Second World War period recipe book from Buchan also advocated making scones by mixing cold porridge and flour, flavouring with syrup, and baking on a hot girdle.

Porridge was often referred to as 'they' or 'them', a usage no doubt derived from the plurality of oats rather than the cooked, singular product. For some people it was also customary to stand whilst eating 'them', but it is not known if this had any significance other than as an aid to digestion, based on an old saying; 'a staunin sack fills the fu'est'.

Many of these 'traditions' were set down by nine-teenth, or early twentieth century cookery writers whose research was often based on oral sources. They will therefore have some substance although it is hard to imagine poor people throughout the land observing such niceties to the letter.

There is a tradition too that hardy Scots eat porridge made with salt and only effete southerners eat it with sugar.

A highlander with a sack of oatmeal
and a message that uses the Gaelic
word for porridge: brochan

This may also have roots in a hard economic reality; sugar was a luxury item until 1874 when the tax was removed and, for most people, it was just too expensive. Certainly early recipes aimed at well-to-do people contradict the popular opposition to sugar. This one, for 'Oatmeal Hasty Pudding', comes from a book, *The Art of Cookery Made Plain and Easy* by Mrs Hannah Glasse, first published in Edinburgh in 1747:

> Take a quart of water, set it to boil, put in a piece of butter and some salt: then, when it boils, with a wooden spoon in one hand and the oatmeal in the other, stir the oatmeal in till it is of a good thickness. Let it boil a few minutes, pour it into your dish, and stick pieces of butter in it: eat with wine and sugar, or ale and sugar, or cream, or new milk.

This dish is similar to the porridge of today, but not the same and another of Mrs Glasse's recipes, for Water-Gruel, offers a variation:

> You must take a pint of water and a large spoonful of oatmeal; then stir it together and let it boil up three or four times, stirring it often. Don't let it boil over, then strain it through a sieve, salt it

to your palate, put in a good piece of fresh butter,
brew it with a spoon till the butter is all melted,
then it will be fine and smooth and very good.
Some love a little pepper in it.

In her legendary *Book of Household Management*
published in 1861, Mrs Beeton suggests 'there are many
ways of making porridge', and lists three:

The one generally adopted – although by no
means the best – is to sprinkle the oatmeal into
boiling, slightly salted water with the left hand,
meanwhile stirring briskly with a wooden spoon
or wooden spatula. When the porridge is thick
enough the stewpan is drawn to the side of the
fire, and the contents slowly cooked from 20 to 30
minutes, being occasionally stirred to prevent it
sticking to the bottom of the pan.

A better method is to soak four ounces of oatmeal
in one and half pints of cold water overnight, and
in the morning strain the water into a stewpan
and, when boiling, add the oatmeal and salt to
taste. Twenty minutes gentle simmering will
sufficiently cook it and it must be well stirred
during the process.

Probably the best plan of all is to use a water-jacketed saucepan for making porridge, for it is always desirable to have oatmeal thoroughly cooked, and as the water in the outer pan obviates the necessity of frequent stirring, the porridge may, with little trouble, be cooked for two or three hours on the previous day, and reheated when required; a pinch of salt should always be added to the porridge.

Warne's *Model Cookery and Housekeeping Book*, a contemporary of Mrs Beeton's weighty tome, also had a recipe for porridge:

Ingredients: Two ounces of oatmeal; one pint of water; half a pint of cold milk.

Method: Put a pint of warm water into a stewpan over the fire, and as it boils dredge in the oatmeal with your left hand and stir with the right. When it is made, turn it into a soup-plate, adding a little salt or a little sugar, according to taste. Send it to table with a jug of hot milk, which should be added to it by degrees for eating.

Sugar and hot milk were guaranteed to raise Scottish hackles, and although Warne's declared aim was to meet the 'requirements of the middle classes of English society', this book and Mrs Beeton's stirred up a hornet's nest as surely as any spurtle or theevil could.

In 1876 the General Assembly of the Church of Scotland set up a committee on Christian Life and Work which reported:

> there is a great need in Scotland of a literature
> dealing with the practical wants of life, to instruct
> men and women in household and domestic
> duties, and in the laws of health and cleanliness.

The women's magazine, the *People's Friend*, took up the challenge and, in 1877, produced a little book with a long title: *THE SCOTTISH COOKERY BOOK* containing *GUID PLAIN RULES for MAKIN' GUID PLAIN MEATS suitable for SMA' PURSES, BIG FAMILIES AND SCOTCH STOMACHS.*

The book's introduction did not mince its words, thundering (as only the People's Friend could): 'No English cook appears capable of producing a single Scotch dish'. It went on:

> Warne's and Beeton's penny Cookery books have
> met with great success in England . . . but to
> Scotch people are practically useless . . . the

recipes given in such books, even for porridge, being simply laughable.

Our little 'Scotch' tome then described the making of porridge:

> To make a really good porridge the water should always have come to the boiling point before the meal is put in; then the meal should be poured regularly in from the hand in a continuous stream, stirring the water all the time. In this consists the high art of porridge making, as on its being well done depends the absence of all unpalatable lumps, and its smoothness and appearance when dished. Allow the porridge to boil ten minutes, stirring frequently, and then put in the salt. It is best not to put in the salt till the end of ten minutes as it has a tendency to harden the meal, and prevent its fully expanding, so that the quality of the porridge is deteriorated. After the salt has been put in, boil for another ten minutes, then dish, and, when provided with good milk you have a 'dainty dish to set before a king'. The consistency of the porridge can be regulated according to the taste of the cook, by putting in less or more meal.

Astute observers will find little difference between this recipe and Mrs Beeton's, but the *People's Friend* writers, schooled in Dundee's famed traditions of journalism, were not going to let inconvenient little truths get in the way of their good English-bashing story.

Another Dundee source, John Grant, whose Craig Mills, Strathmartine, made Grant's Scotch Oatmeal, published their recipe for porridge in 1883:

> Into 6 gills boiling water pour gently from the left
> hand four ounces of Grant's Scotch Oatmeal
> stirring all the time to prevent the meal from
> knotting; salt to taste; boil gently half-an-hour,
> stirring occasionally. Serve with good milk.

For an essentially simple dish, these recipes took time to prepare, but Mrs Beeton's double boiler and the advent of the solid fuel stove provided less labour intensive ways of making porridge. The ingredients were mixed in a pot which was put on the stove or in the oven overnight to cook slowly. Porridge could also be part-cooked the previous night and the pot kept hot in a warm oven or wrapped in hay to retain the heat – as done by the Kirkudbrightshire farmer's wife. (p. 20/21)

In her classic work, *The Scots Kitchen: Its Traditions*

and Lore With Old-Time Recipes, F. Marian McNeill sets out the 'One and Only Method' and advises her readers to 'keep a goblet exclusively for making porridge':

> Allow for each person one breakfastcupful of water, a handful of oatmeal, (about an ounce and a quarter), and a salt-spoonful of salt. Use fresh spring water and be particular about the quality of oatmeal. Midlothian oats are unsurpassed the world over.
>
> Bring the water to the boil and as soon as it reaches boiling point add the oatmeal, letting it fall in a steady rain from the left hand and stirring it briskly the while with the right, sun-wise, or the right hand turn for luck – and convenience. A porridge stick, called a spurtle, and in some parts a theevil, or, as in Shetland, a gruel-tree, is used for the purpose. Be careful to avoid lumps unless the children clamour for them. When the porridge is boiling steadily, draw the mixture to the side and put on the lid. Let it cook for from twenty to thirty minutes, according to the quality of the oatmeal, and do not add the salt, which has a tendency to harden the meal and prevent it

> swelling, until it has cooked for at least ten
> minutes. On the other hand never cook porridge
> without salt.

Her notes accompanying the recipe no doubt raised a few Scottish eyebrows:

> Children often like a layer of sugar, honey, syrup
> or treacle, or of raw oatmeal on top. A morsel of
> butter in the centre of the plate agrees with some
> digestions better than milk.

Janet Murray, in her cookery book published in Aberdeen in 1944, also recognised that there were many ways to make porridge. She wrote of people cooking it for ten minutes, thirty minutes, or even two hours; some stirred the oatmeal quickly into boiling water, others soaked it in cold water overnight; and salt could be added before, during or after cooking. Her own method was to bring a pint of water to the boil, sprinkle in two ounces of meal, stirring all the time, salt to taste and cook gently for an hour.

School domestic science books did not agree either. Published in 1939, Glasgow Corporation Education Department's school cookery book contained a section on 'Invalid Dishes' which included porridge made with one ounce of oatmeal, half a pint of water and salt. The recipe advocated blending the meal with the water and leaving overnight, and after initial cooking leaving the pot to simmer gently for about three-quarters of an hour (by which time the invalid might have got better, or infinitely worse!). Dundee's equivalent, *The Dundee Homecraft Book*, advocated the same proportions of ingredients, but overnight soaking was optional and the cooking and simmering time was about half that for porridge made in Glasgow.

Since the publication of these simple little books a vast array of colourful, glossy cookery books has poured off the presses although few contain original recipes and some bear an uncanny resemblance to those that have gone before. Most people, however, are likely to use the recipe on a rolled oats packet although even these seem to offer as many variations as there are brands on the market. Former Army cook Graham Dunn offers this recipe for a 'beautiful creamy porridge':

> One part rolled oats to two parts water: put oats
> into one part cold water, stir thoroughly and put
> to stand overnight. In the morning, boil remaining
> water and add it to the mixture. Stir, salt to taste,
> simmer for three minutes and serve.

The combinations appear endless. Even so passions can still be stirred (clockwise of course). In the summer of 2003 *The Scotsman* newspaper reviewed *The Good Scots Diet* by Maisie Steven, and included the book's recipe for 'Traditional Scottish Porridge'. It triggered some letters to the editor offering different versions of 'proper', 'perfect', or 'perfect proper' porridge which simply underlined the fact that porridge can be made in many ways. Thus, in so staunchly advocating their own particular method, these correspondents may unwittingly have hit on the real tradition: that each individual porridge-eater can cook it the way they want and eat it any which way they choose. Enjoy!

SOURCES

A number of books and periodicals were consulted in the author's research. These included:

Adams, David G. *Bothy Nichts and Days* 1991

Beeton, Isabella *Household Management* 1861

Brown, Catherine *Scottish Cookery* 1985

Corporation of Glasgow *School Cookery Book* 1939

Dundee Domestic Science Teachers *Dundee Homecraft Book* (1940s)

Gauldie, Enid *The Scottish Country Miller 1700-1900* 1981

Findlay, William M. *Oats: Their Cultivation and Use from Ancient Times to the Present Day* 1956

Lockhart, Wallace *The Scot And His Oats* 1983 (retitled and reprinted 1997)

Mabey, David *In Search of Food* 1978

McNeill, F. Marian *The Scots Kitchen: Its Traditions and Lore With Old Time Recipes* 1929 (plus subsequent reprints)

Murray, Janet *Janet Murray's Cookery Book* 1944

People's Friend *The Scottish Cookery Book* 1877

Peterson, Vicki *The Natural Food Catalogue* 1978

Plant, Marjorie *The Domestic Life of Scotland in the 18th Century* 1952

Seymour, John *The Complete Book of Self-Sufficiency* 1976

Smout, T.C. *A History of the Scottish People 1560-1830* 1969

Steel, Tom *The Life and Death of St Kilda* 1975

Steven, Maisie *The Good Scots Diet* 1985 (new edition 2003)

Stobart, Tom *The Cook's Encyclopaedia* 1980

The Glasgow Herald (various dates)

The Miller (various dates)

The Scottish National Dictionary

Westland, Pamela *Oat Cuisine* 1985

WEB SITES

www.goldenspurtle.com

www.hamlynsoats.co.uk

www.oatmealofalford.co.uk

www.quakeroatmeal.com

Acknowledgements

The following are due thanks for their help with this book:
the staff of the Mitchell Library in Glasgow;
the Edinburgh Room of the Edinburgh City Library;
Dundee City Library;
Cupar Library;
Dr Anthony Morton, Archivist to The Royal Logistical
Corps Museum;
Ian Miller of Hogarth Mills, Kelso;
Quaker Oats, Uthrogle Mills, Cupar;
Peter Mackinnon of Elmwood College, Cupar;
Dorothy Wedderburn of Carrbridge Community Council;
Colonel Paul Budd OBE;
Graham R. Dunn; Morris Wilson; Jean Dewar;
Liz Coogans; Roslyn Anderson; David Torrie;
Roy Galloway and all the dealers in old picture postcards
who joined in the hunt for illustrations.

Other books from Argyll Publishing

The Good Scots Diet
Maisie C Steven
ISBN:1 902831 54 3 £6.99 paperback

'She raids the past for nutritional wisdom.'
The Herald

'Steven has drawn on a lifetime of experience.'
The Scotsman

Until the industrial age, the diet of ordinary people in Scotland was good. Just what happened to diet when the rural populations of Scotland and Ireland flooded into the industrial cities? And how has this led to such poor dietary habits in the modern age with such drastic consequences for health?

Masie Steven has researched the history of Scotland's diet and examines current eating habits. Learning from the best practices of the past, she makes a series of simple and practical suggestions for healthy eating, with a number of short recipes for wholesome traditional meals.

www.argyllpublishing.com